Succeeding with the Masters®
THE FESTIVAL COLLECTION®

Compiled and edited by HELEN MARLAIS

About the Series

Welcome to *The Festival Collection*®! This nine-volume series is designed to give students and teachers a great variety of fabulous repertoire from the Baroque, Classical, Romantic, and Twentieth/Twenty-First Centuries. The series is carefully leveled from early elementary through advanced repertoire. These pieces are true crowd pleasers and will showcase students' technical and musical abilities. Each level covers the gamut of your repertoire needs, from works that showcase power and bravura, to pieces that develop a student's sense of control and finesse. Having a wide selection of works with pedagogically-correct leveling will help make your repertoire selections easier and your students' performances more successful.

Each book includes a CD recording of all of the corresponding works to guide students in their interpretation. The editing in the scores reflects these CD performances. While the CD performances are consistent with the editing in the books, and vice versa, they also demonstrate an appropriate degree of interpretive license. My goal is to instill an appreciation for accurate performances, while nurturing a sense for stylistically appropriate interpretive license. Books one through six were recorded by Helen Marlais, and books seven and eight were recorded by Helen Marlais, Chiu-Ling Lin, and Frances Renzi, giving students at these higher levels the opportunity to hear three different performance styles.

The Festival Collection® is a companion series to the *Succeeding with the Masters*® series. *Succeeding with the Masters*® provides the student with practice strategies and valuable information about the musical characteristics of each era. *The Festival Collection*® expands the repertoire selection with numerous additional top-drawer pedagogical works in a wide array of styles, and with different musical and technical demands. There is no duplication of repertoire between these two series. All of the pieces in both series are motivational and exciting for students to learn as well as for teachers to teach!

Enjoy the series!

Helen Marlais

THE FJH MUSIC COMPANY INC.
Frank J. Hackinson

Production: Frank J. Hackinson
Production Coordinator: Philip Groeber
Cover Design and Art Direction: Gwen Terpstra, Terpstra Design, San Francisco, CA, in collaboration with Helen Marlais
Illustration: Keith Criss, TradigitalWorks, Oakland, CA
Engraving: Tempo Music Press, Inc.
Printer: Tempo Music Press, Inc.

ISBN-13: 978-1-56939-564-6

2

The Festival Collection® Book 1

Era	Composer	Title	Page	CD Track
BAROQUE				
BAROQUE	Praetorius, Michael	Old German Dance	6	1
BAROQUE	Schein, Johann Hermann	Allemande	7	2
BAROQUE	Hove, Joachim van den	Canary	8	3
BAROQUE	Geoffroy, Jean-Nicolas	Petit Minuet	9	4
BAROQUE	Peuerl, Paul	Intrada	10	5
BAROQUE	Geoffroy, Jean-Nicolas	Petit Rondo	11	6
CLASSICAL				
CLASSICAL	Türk, Daniel Gottlob	Minuet	12	7
CLASSICAL	Türk, Daniel Gottlob	A Carefree Fellow	12	8
CLASSICAL	Hook, James	Minuet	13	9
CLASSICAL	Türk, Daniel Gottlob	Sonatina	14	10, 11, 12
CLASSICAL	Diabelli, Anton	Song	16	13
CLASSICAL	Reinagle, Alexander	Allegro	17	14
CLASSICAL	Bach, Johann Christian/ Ricci, Francesco Pasquale	Agitato (T349/1)	18	15

FJH1625

Era	Composer	Title	Page	CD Track

ROMANTIC

Era	Composer	Title	Page	CD Track
ROMANTIC	Gedike, Alexander	A Song (Op. 36, No. 3)	19	16
ROMANTIC	Gurlitt, Cornelius	The Young Dancer (Op. 117, No. 7)	20	17
ROMANTIC	Gurlitt, Cornelius	Kitten Play (Op. 117, No. 9)	21	18
ROMANTIC	Vogel, Moritz	Valsette	22	19
ROMANTIC	Spindler, Fritz	Spring Waltz	24	20

20TH/21ST CENTURIES

Era	Composer	Title	Page	CD Track
20TH/21ST CENT	Kutnowski, Martín	Trumpets	26	21
20TH/21ST CENT	Rahbee, Dianne Goolkasian	Snowflakes Gently Falling	27	22
20TH/21ST CENT	Rubbach, A.	The Sparrows	28	23
20TH/21ST CENT	Bartók, Béla	Hungarian Song	29	24
20TH/21ST CENT	Brown, Timothy	Arabian Dance	30	25
20TH/21ST CENT	Frackenpohl, Arthur R.	Air for Southpaw	31	26
20TH/21ST CENT	Salutrinskaya, Tat'iana	The Shepherd Plays	32	27

ABOUT THE PIECES AND THE COMPOSERS   33

The Festival Collection® Book 1

Composer	Title	Theme	Page	CD Track
Bach, Johann Christian / Ricci, Francesco Pasquale	Agitato *(T349/1)*		18	15
Bartók, Béla	Hungarian Song		29	24
Brown, Timothy	Arabian Dance		30	25
Diabelli, Anton	**Song**		16	13
Frackenpohl, Arthur R.	Air for Southpaw		31	26
Gedike, Alexander	A Song *(Op. 36, No. 3)*		19	16
Geoffroy, Jean-Nicolas	Petit Minuet		9	4
Geoffroy, Jean-Nicolas	Petit Rondo		11	6
Gurlitt, Cornelius	Kitten Play *(Op. 117, No. 9)*		21	18
Gurlitt, Cornelius	The Young Dancer *(Op. 117, No. 7)*		20	17
Hook, James	**Minuet**		13	9
Hove, Joachim van den	Canary		8	3
Kutnowski, Martín	Trumpets		26	21

Peuerl, Paul . . . . Intrada 10 5

Praetorius, Michael . . . . Old German Dance 6 1

Rahbee, Dianne Goolkasian . . . . . . Snowflakes Gently Falling 27 22

Reinagle, Alexander . . . . Allegro 17 14

Ricci, Francesco Pasquale /
Bach, Johann Christian . . . . Agitato *(T349/1)* 18 15

Rubbach, A. The Sparrows 28 23

Salutrinskaya, Tat'iana . . . . The Shepherd Plays 32 27

Schein, Johann Hermann . . . . Allemande 7 2

Spindler, Fritz . . . . Spring Waltz 24 20

Türk, Daniel Gottlob . . . . **A Carefree Fellow** 12 8

Türk, Daniel Gottlob . . . . **Minuet** 12 7

Türk, Daniel Gottlob . . . . **Sonatina** . . . .   14 . . 10, 11, 12

Vogel, Moritz . . . . Valsette 22 19

OLD GERMAN DANCE

Michael Praetorius
(1571-1621)

Moderato (♩ = ca. 100)

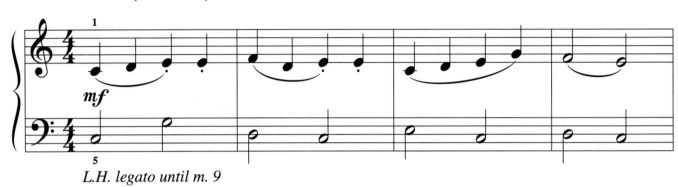

L.H. legato until m. 9

ALLEMANDE

Johann Hermann Schein
(1586-1630)

Allegretto (♩ = ca. 80)

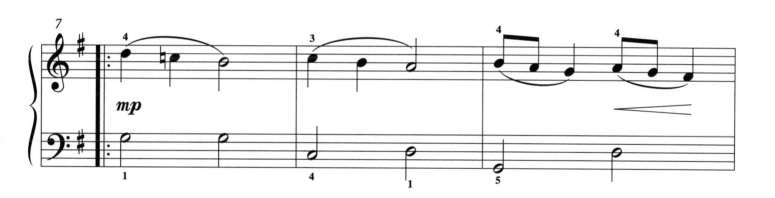

CANARY

Joachim van den Hove
(1567-1620)

Allegro (♩ = ca. 96)

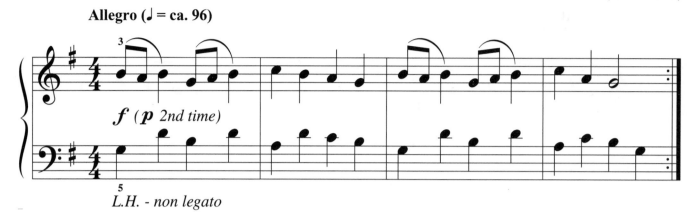

L.H. - non legato

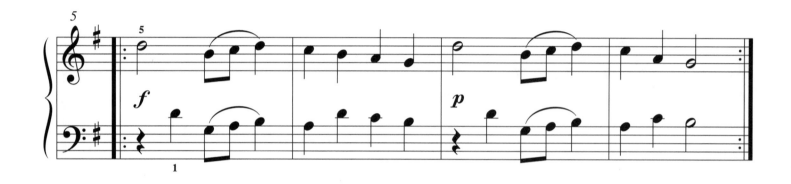

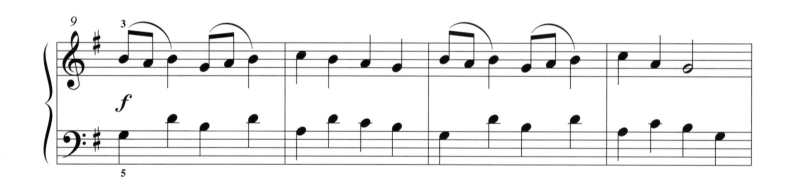

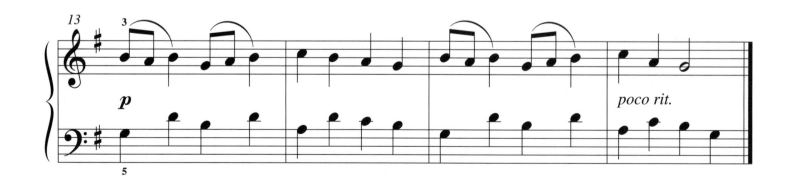

Petit Minuet

Jean-Nicolas Geoffroy
(1633-1694)

Allegro moderato (♩ = ca. 176)

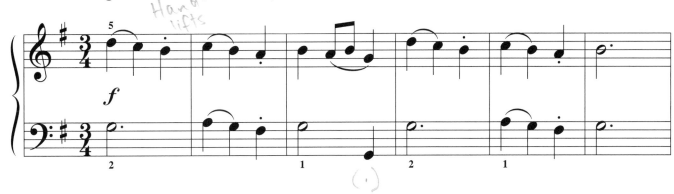

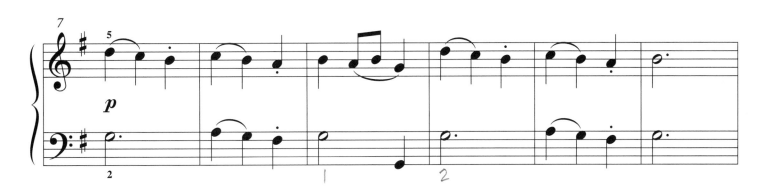

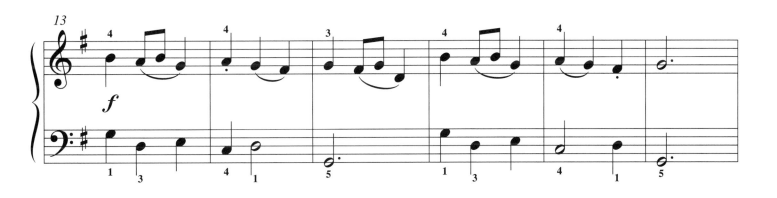

FJH1625

INTRADA

Paul Peuerl
(1570-1625)

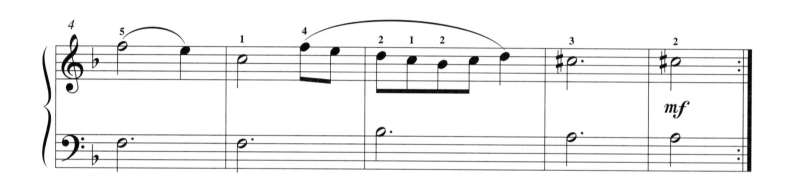

PETIT RONDO

Jean-Nicolas Geoffroy
(1633-1694)

Allegro moderato (♩ = ca. 92)
(a)

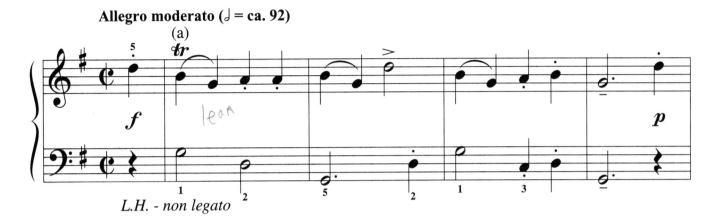

L.H. - non legato

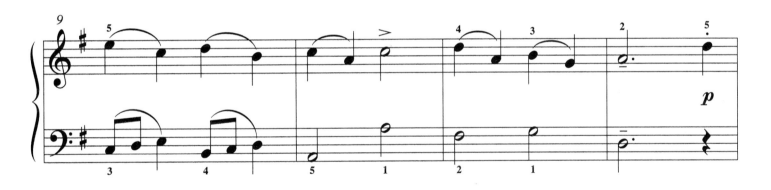

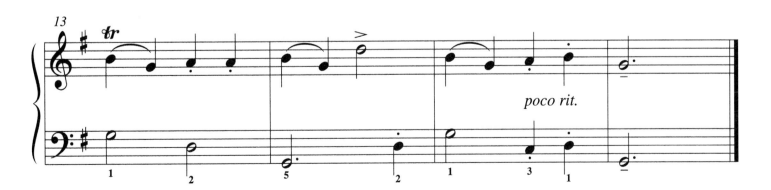

N.B. The trills are optional.　(a)

Minuet

Daniel Gottlob Türk
(1750-1813)

Allegretto (♩ = ca. 168)

A Carefree Fellow

(Un sans-souci)

Daniel Gottlob Türk
(1750-1813)

Allegro moderato (♩ = ca. 88)

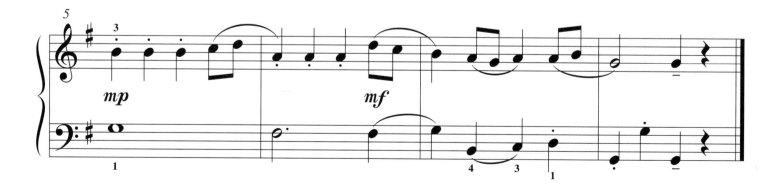

Minuet

James Hook
(1746-1827)

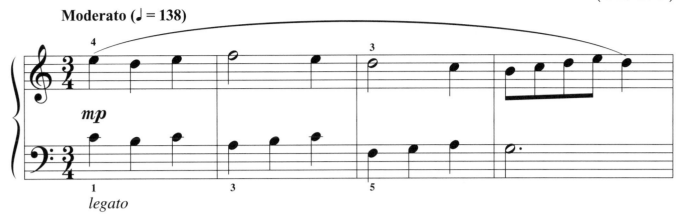

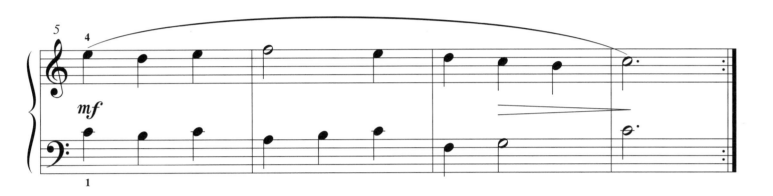

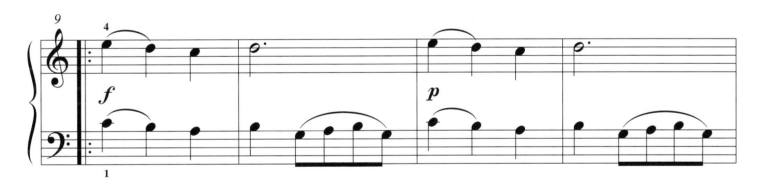

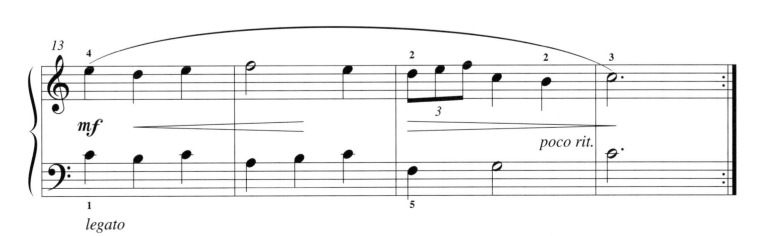

SONATINA

Daniel Gottlob Türk
(1750-1813)

I

III

Allegro (♩ = 100-112)

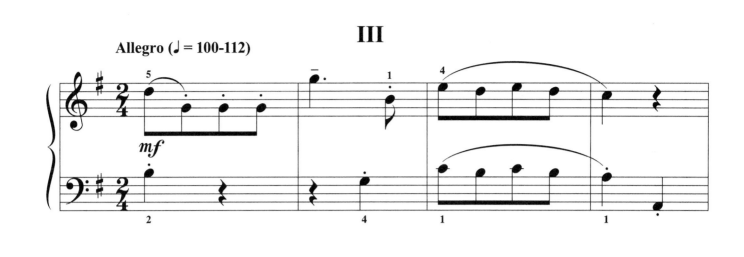

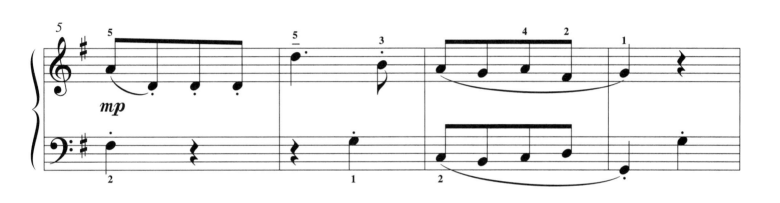

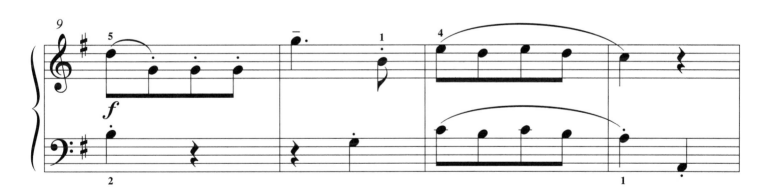

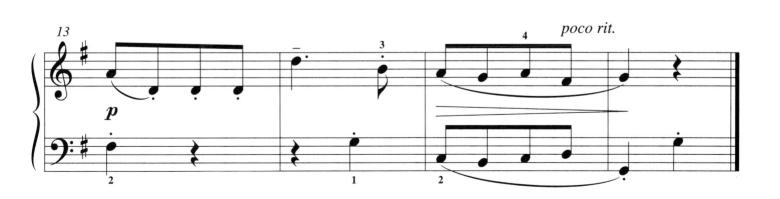

Song

Anton Diabelli
(1781-1858)

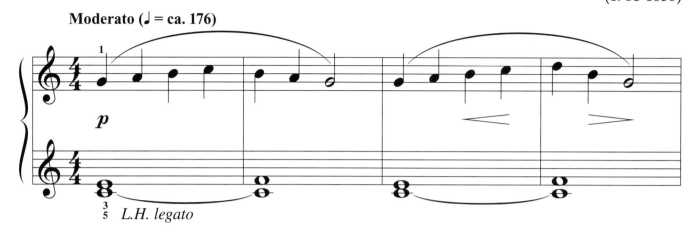

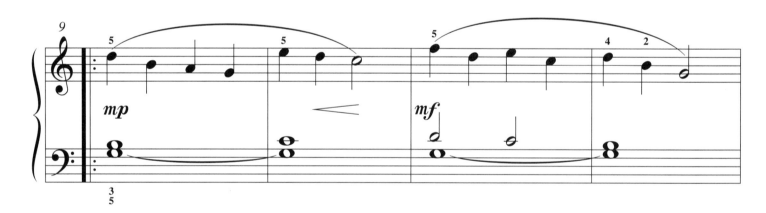

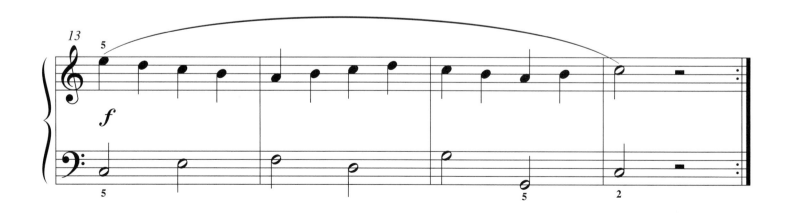

FJH1625

ALLEGRO

Alexander Reinagle
(1756-1809)

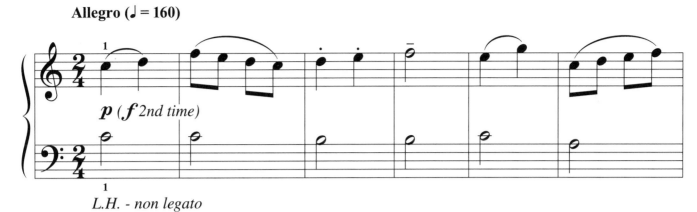

FJH1625

AGITATO

(T349/1)

Johann Christian Bach
(1735-1782)
Francesco Pasquale Ricci
(1732-1817)

Briskly (♩ = ca. 126)

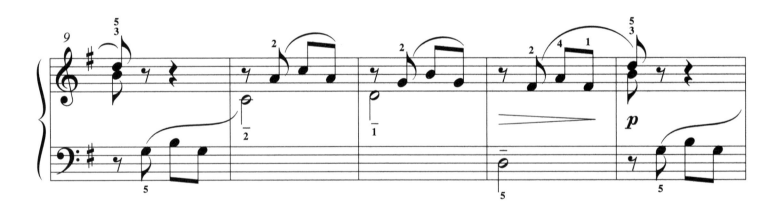

A Song

(Opus 36, No. 3)

Alexander Fyodorovich Gedike
(1877-1957)

Allegro moderato (♩ = ca. 192)

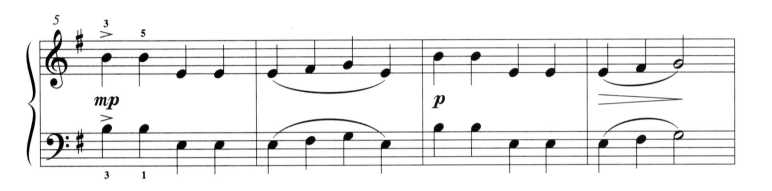

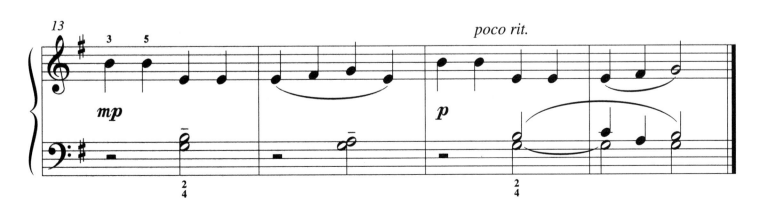

THE YOUNG DANCER

(Opus 117, No. 7)

Cornelius Gurlitt
(1820-1901)

KITTEN PLAY

(Opus 117, No. 9)

Cornelius Gurlitt
(1820-1901)

VALSETTE

Moritz Vogel
(1846-1922)

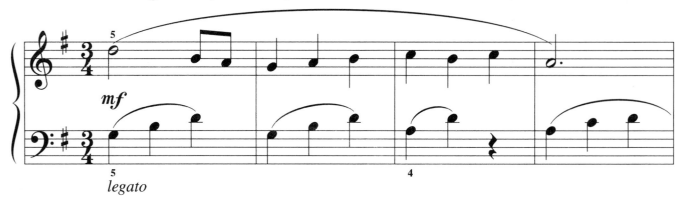

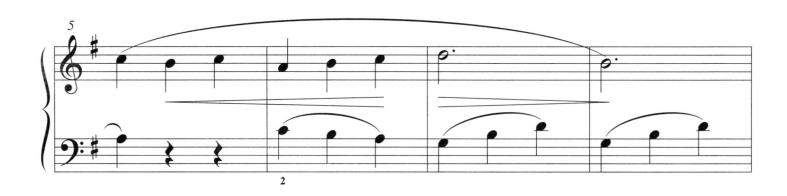

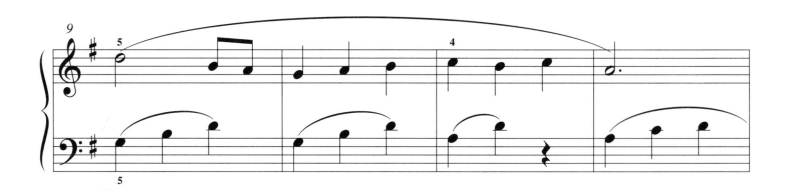

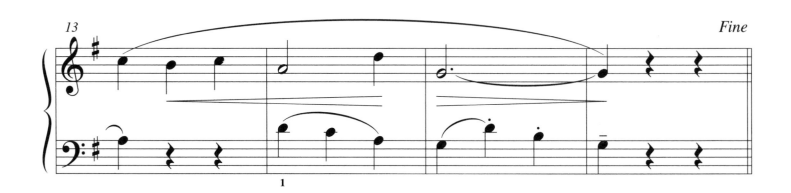

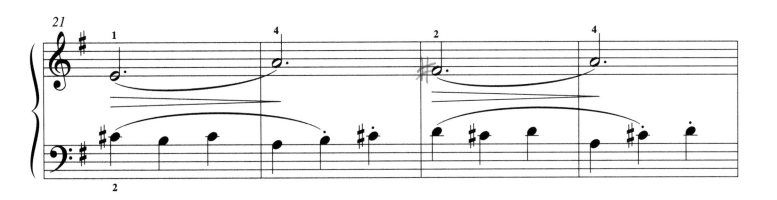

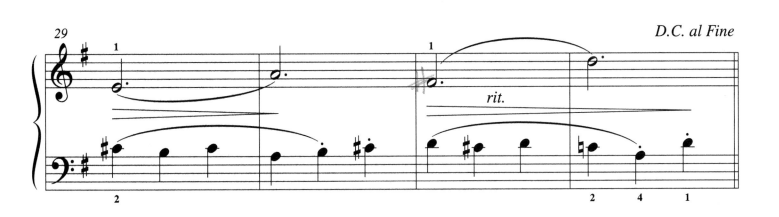

SPRING WALTZ

Fritz Spindler
(1817-1905)

Allegretto (♩ = ca. 168)

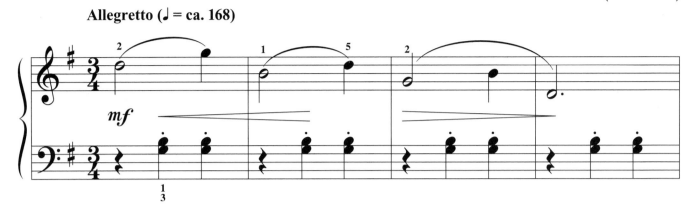

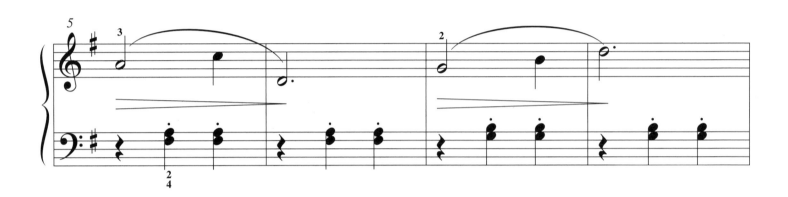

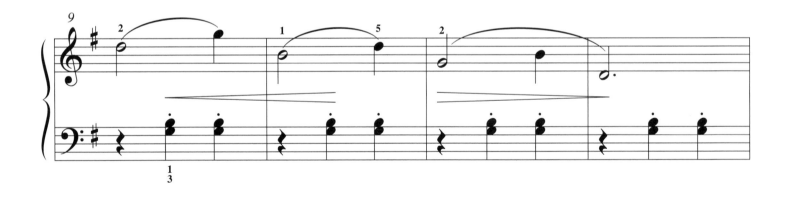

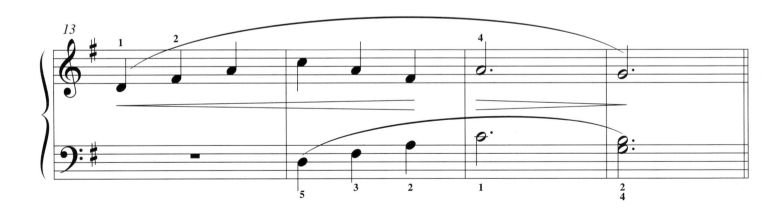

TRUMPETS

from *Echoes, Pictures, Riddles, and Tales for Piano Solo*

Martín Kutnowski
(1968-   )

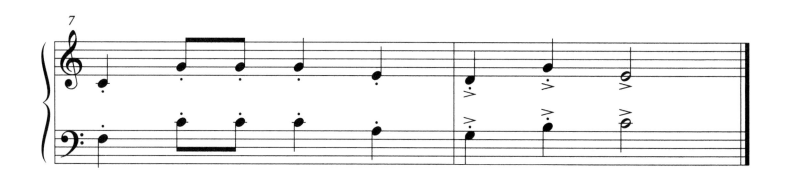

SNOWFLAKES GENTLY FALLING

from *Pictures and Beyond*

Dianne Goolkasian Rahbee
(1938-   )

FJH1625

THE SPARROWS

A. Rubbach
(20th Century)

Giocoso (♩ = 120)

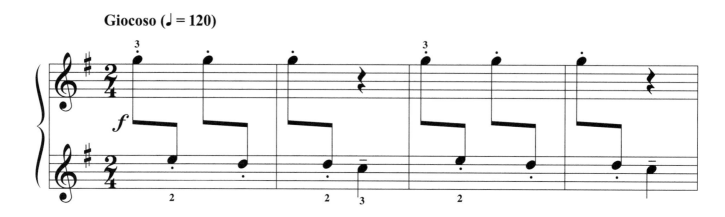

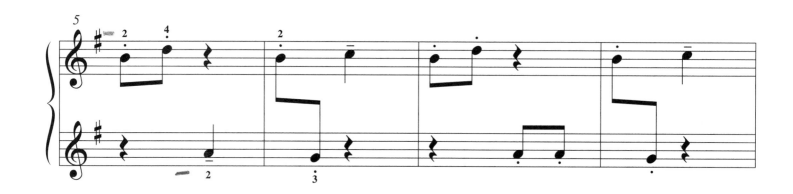

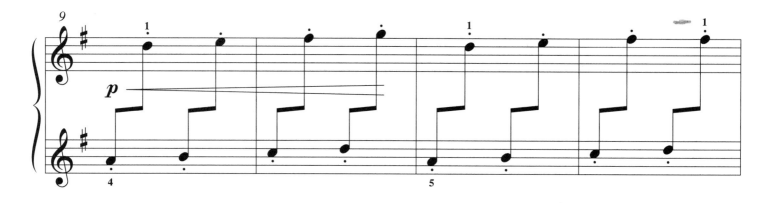

HUNGARIAN SONG

from *First Term at the Piano*

Béla Bartók
(1881-1945)

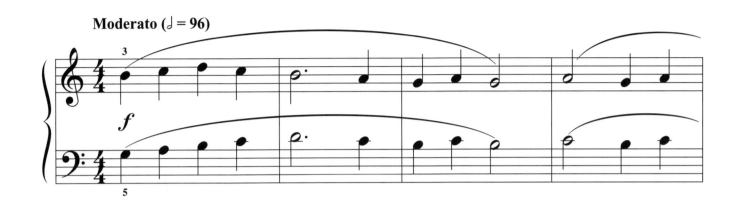

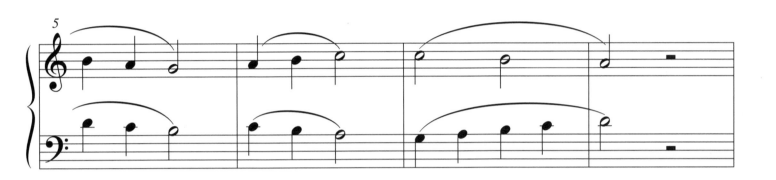

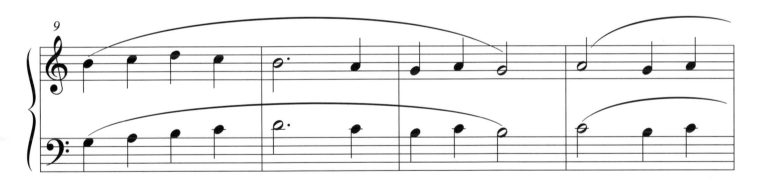

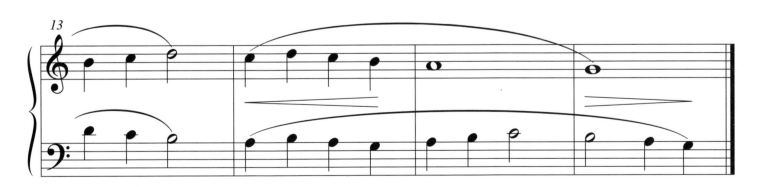

FJH1625

ARABIAN DANCE

Timothy Brown
(1959-   )

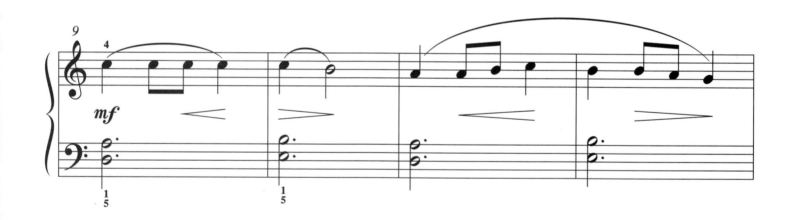

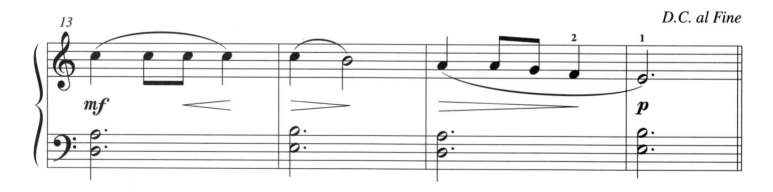

AIR FOR SOUTHPAW

from *Circus Parade*

Arthur R. Frackenpohl
(1924-   )

FJH1625

THE SHEPHERD PLAYS

Tat'iana Salutrinskaya
(20th Century)

Andante cantabile (♩ = 104)

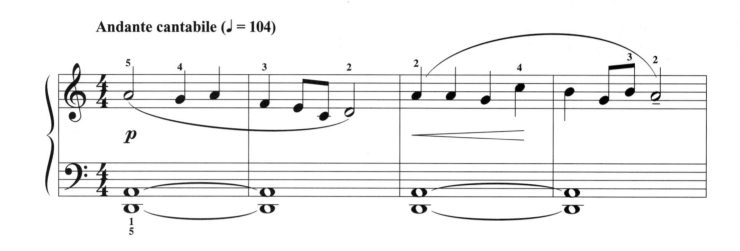

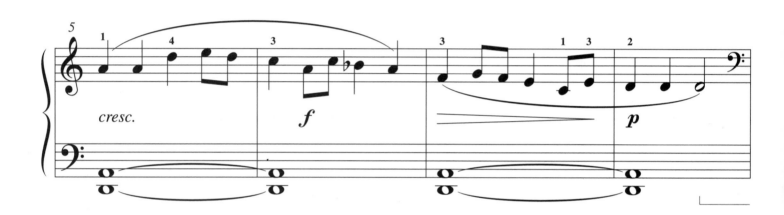

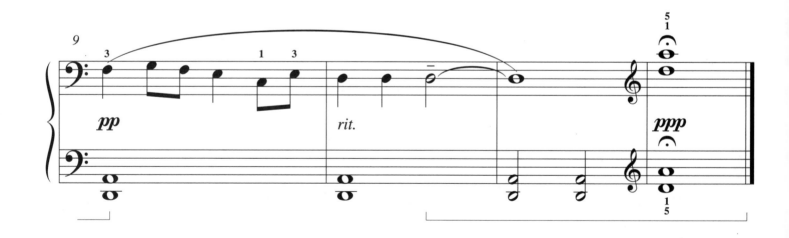

ABOUT THE PIECES AND THE COMPOSERS

BAROQUE ERA

Old German Dance, by Michael Praetorius (1571-1621)
Michael Praetorius was a German composer, writer, organist, and choirmaster. His choral arrangement of the carol *Es ist ein ros entsprungen* is very well known. This piece is an example of a very early dance known as an *allemande*. In German, it would be entitled "Tanz" (dance) or "Deutschertanz" (German dance).

Allemande, by Johann Hermann Schein (1586-1630)
This German composer's instrumental music includes an important collection of dances. An *allemande* was a popular dance during the Baroque era. It was one of the main dances within the baroque suite, along with the *courante*, the *sarabande*, and the *gigue*. Allemandes are usually in duple meter, and there are German, French, and Italian varieties.

Canary, by Joachim van den Hove (1567-1620)
The *canary* is a dance that early sources claim originated in the Canary Islands. Joachim van den Hove was a composer and teacher from the Netherlands. He was also known as a fine lute player. A lute is a stringed instrument with a pear shape. He was a very successful teacher, and this piece was probably a work for lute! Unfortunately he died in poverty after getting into financial difficulties.

Petit Minuet, by Jean-Nicolas Geoffroy (1633-1694)
Geoffroy was a well-known organist who lived in Paris. He is known as the author of the largest collection of harpsichord music of seventeenth-century France. There are manuscript copies of 217 of his pieces for harpsichord, viol, and organ! A *minuet* is a seventeenth- and eighteenth-century dance of French origin, written in triple time.

Intrada, by Paul Peuerl (1570-1625)
Paul Peuerl was a German composer, organist, and organ-builder, who is credited with the invention of the German variation-suite form, which consists of four dances: *paduana, intrada, dance,* and *galliard*. The *dance* is the basic theme, and the other three are variations of it. Three of Peuerl's instrumental collections are known today.

Petit Rondo, by Jean-Nicolas Geoffroy (1633-1694)
Geoffroy held various posts as an organist in Paris, and although he was a fine organist, it is his vast collection of harpsichord works that truly reveals his talent. A *rondo* has a primary section or theme (the "refrain"), and has one or more secondary sections or themes. The most basic rondo has a primary theme first and last with one secondary theme in between (AABA).

FJH1625

CLASSICAL ERA

Minuet, by Daniel Gottlob Türk (1750-1813)
Daniel Gottlob Türk was born in Germany, the son of a manufacturer and secretary to the local mining authority. His father wisely introduced the young Türk to music, and was able to arrange for Daniel to attend the Dresdner Academy, where he received a superior and comprehensive education.

A Carefree Fellow *(Un sans-souci)*, by Daniel Gottlob Türk (1750-1813)
Türk sang in a choir, learning motets and cantatas by J.S. Bach. The talented young man also learned to play the organ. He began his university studies at the age of twenty-two in Leipzig, Germany, where he was introduced to the music of the Baroque era and especially the music of G.F. Handel. He began composing, and his first works were four symphonies, one large choral work, and four cantatas.

Minuet, by James Hook (1746-1827)
The English organist and composer James Hook was one of the most successful and popular musicians of his day. A gifted child, he appeared as a harpsichord soloist at the age of six, and composed a ballad opera at the age of eight. He composed many organ concertos, light music, and over 2,000 songs, as well as a successful comic opera, written with his witty wife.

Sonatina, by Daniel Gottlob Türk (1750-1813)
Türk lectured on music theory at the University in Halle, Germany, and was appointed Music Director of the University, a highly prestigious position. He created a student *Collegium musicum*, which is the Latin name for a group of people organized to make music for pleasure. He also developed the local orchestra, giving weekly concerts of the works of Haydn, Mozart, and Beethoven.

Song, by Anton Diabelli (1781-1858)
The Austrian composer and publisher Anton Diabelli went to Vienna in 1803 as a teacher of piano and guitar, and lived there for the rest of his life. He became known for his arrangements and compositions. He was employed as a proofreader, and began to publish music, which led to a successful career.

Allegro, by Alexander Reinagle (1756-1809)
Reinagle was born to Austrian parents and studied in England. In 1786, at the age of thirty, he arrived in America and became a teacher. He introduced four-hand piano duet music to America, and even taught George Washington's adopted daughter, Nellie! Reinagle wrote two sets of twenty-four "Short and Easy" pieces for students. The *Allegro* reflects his interest in teaching.

Agitato *(T349/1)*, by Johann Christian Bach (1735-1782) and Francesco Pasquale Ricci (1732-1817)

Johann Christian Bach was a composer, the youngest son of Johann Sebastian. Francesco Pasquale Ricci was a successful Italian composer. Ricci's name appears with Bach's in a piano method book published in 1788. It is likely that the two musicians first became acquainted in Milan, Italy. *Agitato* is the Italian term for "agitated."

ROMANTIC ERA

A Song (Opus 36, No. 3), by Alexander Fyodorovich Gedike (1877-1957)

Gedike was a Russian composer and organist. He studied piano at the Moscow Conservatory, and later appeared as a concert pianist. He took classes in chamber music and orchestra, but had no formal training in composition. In his music he became known as the guardian of strict classical traditions of Russian music.

The Young Dancer (Opus 117, No. 7), by Cornelius Gurlitt (1820-1901)

Cornelius Gurlitt was a German pianist and composer. On a visit to Rome, Italy, where his brother was a well-known painter, his talents as a musician were recognized. He was nominated an honorary member of the papal academy *Di Santa Cecilia*. Returning to Altona, Germany, the city of his birth, he began his musical career as a teacher to the daughters of the Duke.

Kitten Play (Opus 117, No. 9), by Cornelius Gurlitt (1820-1901)

Gurlitt became a military bandmaster, church organist, and Royal Music Director. His compositions include two operettas, an opera, some songs, and a great deal of piano music, written primarily for teaching purposes. Perhaps "The Young Dancer" and "Kitten Play" were composed for the enjoyment of his young students.

Valsette, by Moritz Vogel (1846-1922)

Moritz Vogel was born in Sorgau, Silesia. He studied in Leipzig, Germany, and settled there, performing and teaching. He became deeply involved in his teaching career, and prepared a method that eventually spanned from beginning to advanced levels, containing some of his own teaching compositions. A *valsette* is a little waltz.

Spring Waltz, by Fritz Spindler (1817-1905)

The German composer Fritz Spindler lived in Dresden, Germany, where he made his living as a composer, teacher, and concert pianist. His works include a piano concerto, chamber music, and hundreds of salon pieces. He wrote a number of sonatinas (short, simple sonatas), which were popular as teaching material. How does this particular waltz remind you of Spring?

20TH/21ST CENTURIES

Trumpets (from *Echoes, Pictures, Riddles, and Tales for Piano Solo*), by Martín Kutnowski (1968-   )
Martín Kutnowski is an Argentinian composer and music theorist. In his works he often uses the folk materials of his country. He has written pieces in a range from solo instrumental to orchestral works. He has taught in America, and given lectures on music in the United States, China, Argentina, and Spain.

Snowflakes Gently Falling (from *Pictures and Beyond*), by Dianne Goolkasian Rahbee (1938-   )
Dianne Goolkasian Rahbee was born in Boston, Massachusetts, and was trained as a pianist at The Juilliard School of Music and the Salzburg Mozarteum. She taught herself composition. This impressionistic piece uses the whole-tone scale with pedal throughout, creating a picture of *Snowflakes Gently Falling*. It is excellent for practicing a *portato* touch.

The Sparrows, by A. Rubbach (no dates can be found)
Rubbach is a Russian composer who has written many pieces for children. The theme of sparrows is repeated in another of his compositions, "The Chirpy Little Sparrow." He has edited a number of publications, including *Leopold Mozart's Little Music Book for Piano*.

Hungarian Song (from *First Term at the Piano*), by Béla Bartók (1881-1945)
Béla Bartók was a Hungarian composer, pianist, and authority on folk music. He is considered, along with Franz Liszt, to be his country's greatest composer. He was a relentless collector and analyst of folk music, with his interest beginning in 1904, when he heard a Transylvanian-born young girl singing a lovely peasant folk song.

Arabian Dance, by Timothy Brown (1959-)
Timothy Brown studied piano and composition at the University of North Texas, where he received his Master's degree, and is also an award-winning composer for his compositions for harpsichord. The inspiration for Arabian Dance comes from the colorful traditions and history of the Middle East. The mysterious, modal melody suggests the magical appeal of the desert.

Air for Southpaw (from *Circus Parade*), by Arthur R. Frackenpohl (1924-   )
Arthur (Roland) Frackenpohl is an American composer and teacher. He taught at the Crane School of Music in New York from 1949 to 1985. He composed an opera and chamber music, wrote for orchestra, and authored a book on harmonization. A "southpaw" is slang for someone who is left-handed. Can you see why the composer used this name for the title?

The Shepherd Plays, by Tat'iana Salutrinskaya (no dates can be found)
Tat'iana Salutrinskaya is a Russian composer whose works have primarily been written for teaching purposes. She composed a sonatina for piano, as well as a piano concerto that was published in Moscow in 1958 as part of a series entitled "Easy Music for School."